YOUR DAILY DEVOTIONAL BOOK

Your Daily Devotional Book

Copyright © 2020 Keith Banks-Obanor. All rights reserved.

No rights claimed for public domain material, all rights reserved. No parts of this publication may be reproduced, stored in any retrieval system, or transmitted in any form or by any means, electronic, mechanical, recording, or otherwise, without the prior written permission of the author. Violations may be subject to civil or criminal penalties.

Unless stated otherwise, all Scriptures are taken from the King James Version of the Holy Bible.

ISBN: 978-1-63308-627-2 Paperback
        978-1-63308-628-9 Digital

Interior and Cover Design by *R'tor John D. Maghuyop*

1028 S Bishop Avenue, Dept. 178
Rolla, MO 65401

Printed in United States of America

YOUR DAILY DEVOTIONAL BOOK

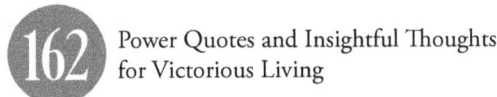 Power Quotes and Insightful Thoughts for Victorious Living

Keith Banks-Obanor
Foreword by Dr. Jerry Grillo

CHALFANT ECKERT
PUBLISHING

TABLE OF CONTENTS

WHAT OTHERS ARE SAYING
ABOUT YOUR DAILY DEVOTION............7

DEDICATION................................9

ACKNOWLEDGMENTS 11

FOREWORD 12

WHY I WROTE THIS
DAILY DEVOTION...........................14

WHAT THIS DAILY DEVOTION
BOOK WILL DO FOR YOU....................15

THE DAILY DEVOTIONS.....................17

ABOUT THE AUTHOR 186

WHAT OTHERS ARE SAYING ABOUT YOUR DAILY DEVOTIONAL

BISHOP G. A. THOMPSON (Author of *Lord, Teach Us to Pray*)

It's an honor to recommend this book. As one of my spiritual sons, Pastor Keith was powerfully used in the gifts of the Spirit when he was part of my congregation. His sound grasp of spiritual truth made him a welcomed voice when the interpretation of spiritual words was necessary. He and his wife, Sogie, were faithful ministers in our church who raised their three children in the nurture and admonition of the Lord, so that all of them are strong believers. This book comes out of Pastor Keith's hunger and thirst after righteousness, and his mature, undying determination to help believers gain a firm grasp of foundational truth. The Daily Devotional words in this book will be a source of spiritual encouragement to all who take the time daily to read and meditate on the devotional words of this book.

Bishop Dr. Gideon Andrew Thompson
Retired Pioneer Pastor: Jubilee Christian Church
Boston, Massachusetts
Senior Prelate: Church Without Walls, International
Headquarters: 1500 Blue Hill Ave., Boston, MA 02126

DR. ANTONIO BURROUGHS, SR.

In an era that is super-paced I am excited to recommend this powerful resource to start the day. This is a devotional like no other; giving timeless biblical life principles to fuel & ignite the passion for success of everyone that reads it. Pastor Keith is an expert in creating momentum and is valued by so many of us. Thanks for this labor of love.

Dr. Antonio Burroughs, Sr.
Founder and President of Antonio
Burroughs International Ministries, Inc.
Weston, Florida

DEDICATION

From the bottom of my heart—I dedicate this Daily Devotional book to my fabulous four—'TEAM BANKS'

- To My Queen, whose love and support are unparalleled. Thanks, Baby, for your commitment to our ministry and our family—thanks for your years of sacrifice and staying home to raise our munchkins. Thank you for being the rock and glue of our family— Love you forever.

- To my princess—My first born—Charisma Banks. You were the first person who put together the first artwork for my book cover. When my vision of being a writer was in its beginning stage and blurry, you created a front page cover that ignited my vision. You helped jumpstart my typing skill, did my page set up, and every imaginary picture backdrop that I ever conceived. You also facilitated part of the book editing and scriptural correction and formatting. You're my high-tech baby—my everything.

- To My Angel—my little heart—Sharon Banks, whose endless commitment, Innovation, and dedication to our music and arts ministry is beyond measure. Your hospitable and given spirit and your sensitivity to the emotional needs of those around you is incomparable. You were born to lead your generation. You'll always be my little heart baby.

- To my one and only son, Jojo, whose praise and worship leadership skill and commitment never cease to amaze me. His ministry has continued to enhance the growth of our music and arts ministry at Victory World Church. You'll always be my buddy.

- Lastly, to Dr. Kitty Bickford who took on this project at the last minute. Your commitment to editing and publishing this book will forever be cherished and highly appreciated. I am forever grateful to God for divinely connecting us.

ACKNOWLEDGMENTS

It would be an unpardonable oversight without the acknowledgment of the following individuals and their contributions in making this project a reality and a dream come through:

- Mr. Herbert G. Chambers—thanks for being one of the lead sponsors of this project, you have been one of my greatest sponsors in every area of my ministry. Your philanthropic spirit is unparalleled. Your entrepreneurship and mentorship in the business world have impacted my life greatly. Thanks Herb!

- A big thank you to the following individuals for their sponsorship and support:

    - Pastors Dexter and Kendra Jenkins
    - Don and Esther Dupie
    - Deborah Francis-Jacob
    - Darlene Knight [Duchess]

FOREWORD

BY DR. JERRY A. GRILLO

I am honored to be allowed the opportunity to write to you about my friend Keith Banks-Obanor. He is a husband, a father, a Pastor and a successful businessman. God has anointed him to lead others out of darkness and into His kingdom light.

In his book, Your Daily Devotional, Pastor Keith Banks-Obanor, has provided 162 keys to assist you in unlocking a full and powerful life. Whether you read one per day or in its entirety, you will be enlightened and stretched to a life of kingdom fulfillment. I would recommend that you take your time and savor every morsel and every crumb of this loaf of wisdom. Taking your time in this read will help you absorb the power of this devotional book.

Pastor Banks has provided several phrases and scriptural references to motivate you and encourage you to continue making wisdom-based decisions. In reality, our whole life is made up of many decisions. Anything that can help you make better ones will eventually help you live a better life.

Each quote will nourish your spiritual man and help you achieve victory through the hustle and bustle of everyday living. I encourage you to remember these keys and scriptures and make this a staple in your daily reading. Write them down. You will not be disappointed.

Remember in the kingdom, sometimes you win and sometimes you learn but you never lose.

>Dr. Jerry A. Grillo
>Founder and Presiding Bishop—Favor Life Church
>Hickory, NC

WHY I WROTE THIS DAILY DEVOTIONAL

I wrote this Daily Devotional book because I realized that we live in a fast-paced society where people don't have the time to sit and read a 300-page book. This book provides you an easy way to find a quick quote or phrase that directly speaks to an area of struggle and difficulty that you face in your life. Now with the Daily Devotional, you can easily access and memorize a life-changing quote or two to chew on as they go about their day.

WHAT THIS DAILY DEVOTIONAL BOOK WILL DO FOR YOU

This Daily Devotional pocket-size book will inspire and motivate you. The simple, insightful quotes in this book are loaded with wisdom for your everyday life application. Every quote will challenge and encourage you as your daily inspirational and spiritual nuggets to nourish your soul and help you live a victorious life through times of difficulties and life challenges. DON'T LEAVE HOME WITHOUT THIS WEALTH OF WISDOM!

THE DAILY DEVOTIONS

Daily Devotion

Never be too quick to make any decision based on your feelings, feelings are temporary—feelings do change, sometimes some feelings may lie to you. But faith and hope in God will bring you stability and confidence.

> *For we live by faith, not by sight.*
> 2 Corinthians 5:7 (NIV)

Said differently, we walk by faith assurance in the promises of God, and not by our sensory perceptions (what we can see, taste, touch, or smell).

Daily Devotion

You will never know the joy of living until you experience the joy and privilege of giving!

Someone else's miracle is always connected to your obedience to give—what you make happen for another, God will make happen for you.

> *And I have been a constant example of how*
> *you can help those in need by working hard.*
> *You should remember the words of the Lord*
> *Jesus: 'It is more blessed to give than to receive.'*
>
> Acts 20:35 (NLT)

Daily Devotion

You are at your best when you are in the center of your expertise, so stay in your lane, discover what you are good at. and value your difference from another.

For by the grace given me I say to every one of you: Do not think of yourself more highly than you ought, but rather think of yourself with sober judgment, in accordance with the faith God has distributed to each of you. For just as each of us has one body with many members, and these members do not all have the same function, so in Christ we, though many, form one body, and each member belongs to all the others. We have different gifts, according to the grace given to each of us. If your gift is prophesying, then prophesy in accordance with your faith; if it is serving, then serve; if it is teaching, then teach; if it is to encourage, then give encouragement; if it is giving, then give generously; if it is to lead, do it diligently; if it is to show mercy, do it cheerfully.

Romans 12:3-8 (NIV)

Daily Devotion

Find your passion and embrace it—even when it may look like you are not making any head-way. If you stay long enough, without fainting—in the pursuit of your passion, you will eventually reap the reward of your labor.

> *Let us not become weary in doing good, for at the proper time we will reap a harvest if we do not give up.*
>
> Galatians 6:9 (NIV)

Another translation says if you do not faint.

Daily Devotion

Crises are inevitable on your way to a place called destiny—but endurance will enable you to experience the miracle on the other side of your journey.

> *Looking unto Jesus the author and finisher of our faith; who for the joy that was set before him endured the cross, despising the shame, and is set down at the right hand of the throne of God.*
>
> Hebrews 12:2 (NKJV)

Daily Devotion

Never re-write your theology to accommodate your flaws and short-comings! Let the word of God be the standard that you measure up to! The Lord admonishes Joshua:

> *Keep this Book of the Law always on your lips; meditate on it day and night, so that you may be careful to do everything written in it. Then you will be prosperous and successful.*
>
> Joshua 1:8 (NIV)

Daily Devotion

You cannot correct or change anything you are willing to put up with—if you keep tolerating it, you'll keep giving life to it. Kill it or live with it.

> *Therefore, if anyone is in Christ, he is a*
> *new creation; old things have passed away;*
> *behold, all things have become new.*
>
> 2 Corinthians 5:17 (NKJV)

Daily Devotion

Do not lose sleep over people that disregard your counsel and mentorship. Don't give your time to people that do not value your insight and wisdom.

> *Don't waste your breath on fools, for*
> *they will despise the wisest advice.*
>
> Proverbs 23:9 (NLT)

Daily Devotion

Never write anyone off from your life until they prove foolish and stop valuing your friendship and relationship.

> *A man of many companions may come to ruin, but there is a friend who sticks closer than a brother.*
>
> Proverbs 18:24 (ESV)

10

Daily Devotion

Do not be too quick to judge and give up on people—give them some space and some time to change, perhaps they will eventually come around! It took you some time to get your act together, too.

> *for though a righteous man falls*
> *seven times, he will rise again, but*
> *the wicked stumble into calamity.*

Proverbs 24:16 (ISV)

Daily Devotion

Time is not always your best friend—you won't always feel inspired or motivated—so take advantage of today's creativity. Give attention and time to develop the ideas that you sense at every given season.

> *There is a time for everything, and a season for every activity under the heavens*
>
> Ecclesiastes:1 (NIV)

Daily Devotion

You can only get out of life what you put into life—so start a savings account today with the bank of hard work and diligence.

> *For thou shalt eat the labour of*
> *thine hands: happy shalt thou be,*
> *and it shall be well with thee.*
>
> Psalm 128:2 (KJV)

> *The desire of the lazy man kills him,*
> *For his hands refuse to labor.*
>
> Proverbs 21:25 (NKJV)

Daily Devotion

Stop waiting for something to happen—start making things happen. No one can be more passionate about your vision than you.

The Just Live by Faith
Then the Lord answered me and said:
Write the vision
And make it plain on tablets,
That he may run who reads it…

Habakkuk 2:2 (NKJV)

Do you see a man diligent in his
business? He will stand before kings; he
will not stand before obscure men.

Proverbs 22:29 (MEV)

Daily Devotion

Stop blaming people for your failures —they've also been to the university of trials and affliction too—but they did not quit.

Many are the afflictions of the righteous, But the LORD delivers him out of them all.

Psalm 34:19 (NKJV)

DAILY DEVOTION

Life will never give you what you deserve—life will always give you what you demand and pursue—so use your faith to demand something out of life.

> *For in it the righteousness of God is revealed from faith to faith; as it is written,"The just shall live by faith."*
> Romans 1:17 (NKJV)

Daily Devotion

Do not let people's opinion about you create in you a feeling of unworthiness

—she says

—he says

—but what does God say about you

> *But now, this is what the Lord says – he who created you, Jacob, he who formed you, Israel: 'Do not fear, for I have redeemed you; I have summoned you by name; you are mine. When you pass through the waters, I will be with you; and when you pass through the rivers, they will not sweep over you. When you walk through the fire, you will not be burned; the flames will not set you ablaze.*
>
> Isaiah 43:1-2 (NIVUK)

Daily Devotion

It's never too late to pick up your dream from where you gave up on it—God is a God of new beginnings and a God of another chance—so you can begin again.

*Forget the former things; do not dwell on
the past. See, I am doing a new thing!
Now it springs up; do you not perceive
it? I am making a way in the wilderness
and streams in the wasteland.*

Isaiah 43:18-19 (NIVUK)

18

Daily Devotion

You can't give up now—you have gone too far to give up! The disgrace of going backwards is far greater than the fear of going forward.

Let us not become weary in doing good, for at the proper time we will reap a harvest if we do not give up.

Galatians 6:9 (NIV)

And let us not be weary in well doing: for in due season we shall reap, if we faint not.

Galatians 6:9 (KJV)

Daily Devotion

Stop comparing yourself with anyone—you are different from everyone. You are uniquely designed, made by God, and simply in a class all by yourself. Your destiny is not an open memo for all to scrutinize and judge.

Before I formed you in the womb I knew you,
before you were born I set you apart;
I appointed you as a prophet to the nations.

Jeremiah 1:5 (NIV)

Daily Devotion

Don't look back now—there's nothing in your past to help you leap forward—keep your eyes straight on the prize.

> *Brothers and sisters, I do not consider myself yet to have taken hold of it. But one thing I do: Forgetting what is behind and straining toward what is ahead, I press on toward the goal to win the prize for which God has called me heavenward in Christ Jesus.*
>
> Philippians 3:13-14 (NIV)

Daily Devotion

Whenever a project or a vision becomes too tough and challenging with endless oppositions, then it must be a sign of how great the rewards and payoffs could be—so keep pulling through.

> *But as for you, be strong and do not give up, for your work will be rewarded.*
> 2 Chronicles 15:7 (NIV)

Daily Devotion

Failure is not a bad thing—it is simply a wake-up call for a rebound.

> *For though the righteous falls*
> *seven times, they rise again,*
>
> Proverbs 24:16 (NIV)

> *Now all glory to God, who is able to*
> *keep you from falling away and will*
> *bring you with great joy into his glorious*
> *presence without a single fault.*
>
> Jude 1:24 (NLV)

> *for all have sinned and fall*
> *short of the glory of God*
>
> Romans 3:23 (NIV)

Daily Devotion

Pain is a sign that the battle is still on and you have a chance to fight fearlessly for victory.

> *No, in all these things we are more than conquerors through him who loved us.*
>
> Romans 8:37 (NIV)

Daily Devotion

Fear paralyzes but faith propels you to go beyond and discover what could be. The fear of the unknown will keep you bound and locked up. Peter exercised faith to step out of the boat.

> *Have I not commanded you? Be strong and courageous. Do not be afraid; do not be discouraged, for the LORD your God will be with you wherever you go.*
>
> Joshua 1:9 (NIV)

Daily Devotion

Don't spend a lifetime grieving over your past mistakes—you can't change your past, but you can create a new future and rewrite your history.

> *Forget the former things; do not dwell on the past. See, I am doing a new thing! Now it springs up; do you not perceive it? I am making a way in the desert and streams in the wasteland.*

Isaiah 43:18-19 (NIV)

Daily Devotion

God will never consult your past to give you a better future, neither will He let your present circumstances intimidate Him or diminish His creative power in you.

for it is God who works in you to will and to act in order to fulfill his good purpose.
Philippians 2:13 (NIV)

27

Daily Devotion

No matter how big your sin, no matter how filthy and dirty you are—God's love is bigger than your sin. His blood washes whiter than snow.

> *"Come now, let us settle the matter," says the LORD. "Though your sins are like scarlet, they shall be as white as snow; though they are red as crimson, they shall be like wool.*
>
> Isaiah 1:18 (NIV)

Daily Devotion

Foolish spending is simply sabotaging your future for your present greed—but delayed gratification is enduring your present to create a desired future. Plan for a future that is far better than your past and present.

> *The wise store up choice food and olive oil, but fools gulp theirs down.*
>
> Proverbs 21:20 (NIV)

> *The plans of the diligent lead to profit as surely as haste leads to poverty.*
>
> Proverbs 21:5 (NIV)

29

Daily Devotion

Stop spending time and energy trying to change other people's opinions. They've been that way before you met them—your few minutes of argument with them won't change a lifetime of ignorance and foolishness.

> *A prudent man conceals knowledge,*
> *but the heart of fools proclaims folly.*
> Proverbs 12:23 (ESV)

Daily Devotion

Stop thinking small, and start thinking big—the bigger your dream, the greater your passion and drive to achieve them.

Now to him who is able to do far more abundantly than all that we ask or think, according to the power at work within us,

Ephesians 3:20 (ESV)

Daily Devotion

Don't kid yourself—habits are not formed in a day. It takes time to form a great habit or bad habit—we become what we consistently give ourselves to—so start forming good habits today.

> *Do not be conformed to this world, but be transformed by the renewal of your mind, that by testing you may discern what is the will of God, what is good and acceptable and perfect.*
>
> Romans 12:2 (ESV)

Daily Devotion

Relationships can only thrive and blossom on the bedrock of commitment, kindness, patience, forgiveness, trust, and a selfless, unconditional love.

*Love is patient, love is kind. It does not envy,
it does not boast, it is not proud.
It does not dishonor others, it is not self-seeking,
it is not easily angered, it keeps
no record of wrongs.
Love does not delight in evil but
rejoices with the truth.
It always protects, always trusts,
always hopes, always perseveres.
Love never fails. But where there
are prophecies, they will cease;
where there are tongues, they will be stilled;
where there is knowledge, it will pass away.*

1 Corinthians 13:4-8 (NIV)

Daily Devotion

Stop demanding a return on an investment that you have not made on any relationship. The reason why you feel hurt and disappointed is because your expectations from people are unrealistic.

> *Do not be deceived: God cannot be mocked. A man reaps what he sows.*
>
> Galatians 6:7 (NIV)

DAILY DEVOTION

Stop being paranoid over the thought that everyone is talking about you or trying to get at you. Trust me when I say that you are not the most important thing on their minds.

For the eyes of the Lord are on the righteous and his ears are attentive to their prayer, but the face of the Lord is against those who do evil.

1 Peter 3:14 (NIV)

Daily Devotion

Stop feeling disappointed whenever people do not respond to your needs quickly. They have a lot on their plates too—and sometimes they perceive their headache to be more important than your heart attack.

> *Nothing should be done because of pride or thinking about yourself. Think of other people as more important than yourself.*
>
> Philippians 2:3 (NLV)

Daily Devotion

Do not hold grudges against anyone for too long, otherwise you'll be holding up your joy and progress while they live in peace.

> *Get rid of all bitterness, rage and anger, brawling and slander, along with every form of malice.*
> *Be kind and compassionate to one another, forgiving each other, just as in Christ God forgave you.*
>
> Ephesians 4:31-32 (NIV)

Daily Devotion

Never hold anyone responsible for your lack of progress in life—God is too smart —too wise—and too creative to place your destiny in the hands of an individual.

> *The man said, "The woman whom*
> *You gave to be with me, she gave*
> *me fruit of the tree, and I ate."*
>
> Genesis 3:12 (NLV)

> *"Why do you look at the speck of sawdust in*
> *your brother's eye and pay no attention to the*
> *plank in your own eye? How can you say to*
> *your brother, 'Let me take the speck out of your*
> *eye,' when all the time there is a plank in your*
> *own eye? You hypocrite, first take the plank out*
> *of your own eye, and then you will see clearly*
> *to remove the speck from your brother's eye.*
>
> Matthew 7:3-5 (NIV)

Daily Devotion

People do change with time through the different seasons of their lives, so go with the flow because you have changed too—but we serve an unchangeable God.

> *Jesus Christ is the same yesterday*
> *and today and forever.*
>
> Hebrews 13:8 (NIV)

> *I the Lord do not change. So you, the*
> *descendants of Jacob, are not destroyed.*
>
> Malachi 3:6 (NIV)

39

Daily Devotion

If we fail to grow together, we'll eventually grow apart. This is true life philosophy—so make up your mind to develop and grow yourself.

Like newborn babies, crave pure spiritual milk, so that by it you may grow up in your salvation,

1 Peter 2:2 (NIV)

When I was a child, I talked like a child, I thought like a child, I reasoned like a child. When I became a man, I put the ways of childhood behind me.

1 Corinthians 13:11 (NIV)

Daily Devotion

Information received increases knowledge. Knowledge gained impacts wisdom and insights. Through insights, we receive revelation which then leads to transformation.

> *For this very reason, make every effort to add to your faith goodness; and to goodness, knowledge;*
>
> 2 Peter 1:5 (NIV)

> *my people are destroyed from lack of knowledge. "Because you have rejected knowledge, I also reject you as my priests; because you have ignored the law of your God, I also will ignore your children.*
>
> Hosea 4:6 (NIV)

Daily Devotion

Fear is a liar—it is an illusion of False Evidence Appearing Real.

> *For God has not given us a spirit of fear, but of power and of love and of a sound mind.*
>
> 2 Timothy 1:7 (NKJV)

Daily Devotion

Your gift will make room for you, but your character will sustain you and lead you into the presence of great men and women.

> *A man's gift makes room for him,*
> *And brings him before great men.*
>
> Proverbs 18:16 (NKJV)
>
> *and endurance produces character,*
> *and character produces hope,*
>
> Romans 5:4 (ESV)

Daily Devotion

Jealousy is for small-minded people. You can never attract into your life whatever you are jealous of or resent. You can only attract what you celebrate. So, celebrate others when you can because your time is coming—you're next in line for a blessing.

> *A heart at peace gives life to the*
> *body, but envy rots the bones.*
>
> Proverbs 14:30 (NIV)

> *And I saw that all toil and all achievement*
> *spring from one person's envy of another. This*
> *too is meaningless, a chasing after the wind.*
>
> Ecclesiastes 4:4 (NIV)

Daily Devotion

You will never leave where you are in life until your mind designs the map for your destination—so look beyond your comfort zone. Peter never knew he could walk on the water until he stepped out of the boat.

Have I not commanded you? Be strong and courageous. Do not be afraid; do not be discouraged, for the Lord your God will be with you wherever you go.

Joshua 1:9 (NIV)

I will lead the blind by ways they have not known, along unfamiliar paths I will guide them; I will turn the darkness into light before them and make the rough places smooth. These are the things I will do; I will not forsake them.

Isaiah 42:16 (NIV)

Daily Devotion

People don't like change because it takes them out of their comfort zone—out of the familiar into the unfamiliar–but understand that your success will always come through the vehicle of change. When God wanted to bless Abraham and make him a father of many nations, He moved him out of his comfort zone: from his father's land–from what he was used to–from the familiar to the unfamiliar.

> *The Lord had said to Abram, "Go from your country, your people and your father's household to the land I will show you. "I will make you into a great nation, and I will bless you; I will make your name great, and you will be a blessing. I will bless those who bless you, and whoever curses you I will curse;*
>
> Genesis 12:1-3 (NIV)

Daily Devotion

Anything alive moves—but stagnation is the enemy of your progress. Stagnation cripples and paralyzes. It's time to move—it's time to go after the dream.

> *Then the Lord answered me and said:*
> *"Write the vision And make it plain on*
> *tablets, That he may run who reads it.*
>
> Habakkuk 2:2 (NKJV)

> *I can do all things through Christ*
> *who strengthens me.*
>
> Philippians 4:13 (NKJV)

Daily Devotion

Always explore every option possible before you draw the conclusion that, "No, it can't be done."

> *Jesus looked at them and said, "With man this is impossible, but with God all things are possible."*
> Matthew 19:26 (NIV)

Daily Devotion

Always be you—don't try to be someone else. Copies are cheap, originals are authentic. Learn from others but be an original. Be comfortable with who you are and whose you are.

> *I praise you, for I am fearfully and wonderfully made. Wonderful are your works; my soul knows it very well. My frame was not hidden from you, when I was being made in secret, intricately woven in the depths of the earth. Your eyes saw my unformed substance; in your book were written, every one of them, the days that were formed for me, when as yet there was none of them.*
>
> Psalm 139:14-16 (ESV)

> *For we are his workmanship, created in Christ Jesus for good works, which God prepared beforehand, that we should walk in them.*
>
> Ephesians 2:10 (ESV)

49

Daily Devotion

Always know what you want—if you don't know what you want out of life, you will settle for anything. You are not an accident existing by chance—God has a plan and a future for you.

> *For I know the plans I have for you, declares the Lord, plans for welfare and not for evil, to give you a future and a hope.*
>
> Jeremiah 29:11 (ESV)

> *And we know that for those who love God all things work together for good, for those who are called according to his purpose.*
>
> Romans 8:28 (ESV)

50

DAILY DEVOTION

Always value and celebrate what you have at every stage and season of your life. An attitude of gratitude and contentment always opens the door for a next level blessing.

*give thanks in all circumstances; for this
is God's will for you in Christ Jesus.*

1 Thessalonians 5:18 (NIV)

*I will give thanks to you, Lord, with all my
heart; I will tell of all your wonderful deeds.*

Psalm 9:1 (NIV)

*I will bless the Lord at all times:
his praise shall continually be in my mouth.*

Psalm 34:1 (KJV)

51

Daily Devotion

Never act like where you are—always act like where you are going. Have a palace mentality even while you are in the pit or prison. Joseph the dreamer did just that in the Book of Genesis.

Jesus also endured the cross for a season, knowing that there is a crown at the end of every cross.

> *Looking unto Jesus the author and finisher of our faith; who for the joy that was set before him endured the cross, despising the shame, and is set down at the right hand of the throne of God.*
>
> Hebrews 12:2 (KJV)

Daily Devotion

Do not put your life on hold when you are waiting patiently for a miracle. Do whatever your hand can find to do in the meantime, and it will surprise you how quickly time can go by. Before you know it, your waiting is over, and opportunity will come knocking at your door.

> *But they who wait upon the Lord will get*
> *new strength. They will rise up with wings*
> *like eagles. They will run and not get tired.*
> *They will walk and not become weak.*
>
> Isaiah 40:31 (NLV)

Daily Devotion

Idle minds and unoccupied hands never attract opportunity. You are a success on your way to somewhere, so get moving.

> *Whatever you do, do well. For when you go to the grave, there will be no work or planning or knowledge or wisdom.*
> Ecclesiastes 9:10 (NLV)

Daily Devotion

Faith is not some mystical illusion or a false imagination, but rather faith is a strong conviction of hope based on the promises that can be found in God's Word. Faith is having a strong sense of what already exists in the spirit realm being made manifest in the physical realm.

> *Now faith is the substance of things hoped for, the evidence of things not seen.*
>
> Hebrews 11:1 (KJV)

Daily Devotion

Accepting and liking people that only look like you is uncivilized and narrow minded—so choose to be color blind.

> *And now these three remain: faith, hope and love. But the greatest of these is love.*
>
> 1 Corinthians 13:13 (NIV)

Daily Devotion

If you are not where you need to be in life yet, do not become frustrated or disappointed.

Keep nurturing the seeds of greatness in you—God is never too late to get to you.

> *being confident of this, that he who began*
> *a good work in you will carry it on to*
> *completion until the day of Christ Jesus.*
>
> Philippians 1:6 (NIV)

Daily Devotion

You will succeed in anything you put your heart to do with total commitment if you do not give up or throw in the towel—especially when you encounter strong opposition, discouragement, and difficulty along the way. Remain diligent!

> *Seest thou a man diligent in his business? he shall stand before kings; he shall not stand before mean men.*
>
> Proverbs 22:29 (KJV)

> *Cast thy burden upon the Lord, and he shall sustain thee: he shall never suffer the righteous to be moved.*
>
> Psalm 55:22 (KJV)

Daily Devotion

Anything that will be great takes time and process. Greatness without process is counterfeit and only a temporary success.

*Knowing this, that the trying of
your faith worketh patience.
But let patience have her perfect work, that ye
may be perfect and entire, wanting nothing.*

James 1:3-4 (KJV)

Daily Devotion

Do not make a permanent decision because of a temporary situation. Your troubles and trials are only for a season.

> ...*Weeping may last for the night, But a shout of joy comes in the morning.*
>
> Psalm 30:5 (NASB)

Daily Devotion

Whatever you give yourself to the most will eventually rule you, pull you, and dominate you—because you are the sum total of the influences you allow into your life.

> *Do not be misled: "Bad company corrupts good character."*
>
> 1 Corinthians 15:33 (NIV)

> *Submit yourselves, then, to God. Resist the devil, and he will flee from you. Come near to God and he will come near to you. Wash your hands, you sinners, and purify your hearts, you double-minded.*
>
> James 4:7-8 (NIV)

61

DAILY DEVOTION

Stop looking back and giving so much thought to your past. There's nothing good back there in your past, only painful memories! Instead, look straight ahead and straight up. Focus on the now and on your future so that you will have endless possibilities!

> *Forget the former things; do not dwell on*
> *the past. See, I am doing a new thing!*
> *Now it springs up; do you not perceive*
> *it? I am making a way in the wilderness*
> *and streams in the wasteland.*
>
> Isaiah 43:18-19 (NIV)

Daily Devotion

Procrastination is an enemy of your destiny and a hindrance of God's blessing, so don't put off anything you can do today. Tomorrow is not promised. Do what you can today that will impact your tomorrow and move you closer to your destiny.

> *Whoever watches the wind will not plant;*
> *whoever looks at the clouds will not reap.*
>
> Ecclesiastes 11:4 (NIV)

> *As long as it is day, we must do the*
> *works of him who sent me. Night is*
> *coming, when no one can work.*
>
> John 9:4 (NIV)

> *Be dressed ready for service and*
> *keep your lamps burning,*
>
> Luke 12:35 (NIV)

> *Lazy hands make for poverty, but*
> *diligent hands bring wealth.*
>
> Proverbs 10:4 (NIV)

63

Daily Devotion

The people that come into your life in one season may not necessarily be there in the next season of your life, so be at peace with it. People come and go.

> *One who has unreliable friends soon*
> *comes to ruin, but there is a friend*
> *who sticks closer than a brother.*
>
> Proverbs 18:24 (NIV)

Daily Devotion

Do not share your dreams and successes with anyone who does not have the capacity, mentality, and a winner's mindset to see beyond their shallow and narrow mindedness. There are dream killers and haters, and there are also dream builders. Stay away from the haters and gravitate towards the builders!

> *Joseph had a dream, and when he told it to his brothers, they hated him all the more.*
>
> Genesis 37:5 (NIV)

65

DAILY DEVOTION

There's always a different wave—a different swing—and a different momentum for every season. The wisdom to know when seasons change is very vital.

> *He changes times and seasons; he deposes kings and raises up others. He gives wisdom to the wise and knowledge to the discerning.*
>
> Daniel 2:21 (NIV)

> *Now learn this lesson from the fig tree: As soon as its twigs get tender and its leaves come out, you know that summer is near. Even so, when you see all these things, you know that it is near, right at the door.*
>
> Matthew 24:32-33 (NIV)

Daily Devotion

Never ignore your instinct—it could save you a lifetime of misery and pain. Pay attention to the impressions that God lays in your spirit man.

The human spirit is the lamp of the Lord that sheds light on one's inmost being.

Proverbs 20:27 (NIV)

Daily Devotion

Do not spend a lifetime functioning in an area or on a job that does not fulfill your life purpose. There's nothing wrong starting somewhere but refuse to remain where you started.

May the favor of the Lord our God rest on us; establish the work of our hands for us—yes, establish the work of our hands.

Psalm 90:17 (NIV)

A sluggard's appetite is never filled, but the desires of the diligent are fully satisfied.

Proverbs 13:4 (NIV)

All hard work brings a profit, but mere talk leads only to poverty.

Proverbs 14:23 (NIV)

Daily Devotion

When you are stressed—tired and discouraged of pursuing your goals and vision—get some rest, take a break, and enjoy a moment to breathe and reflect. But in all that you do, never quit!

Quitting is for failures.

> *Come to me, all you who are weary*
> *and burdened, and I will give you*
> *rest. Take my yoke upon you*
> *and learn from me, for I am gentle and humble*
> *in heart, and you will find rest for your souls.*
>
> Matthew 11:28-29 (NIV)

69

Daily Devotion

At every stage and season of your life's journey, remember to pause for a moment to count your blessings and celebrate your victories. Focusing too much on your struggles and battles often will only lead you to an endless parade of frustrations, a sense of unfulfillment, and depleted energy and motivation.

What shall I render to the Lord For all His benefits toward me?

Psalm 116:12 (NKJV)

Bless the Lord, O my soul, And forget not all His benefits:

Psalm 103:2 (NKJV)

Daily Devotion

Always keep your focus on the main thing—do not try to do everything and end up doing nothing. Always keep your priorities right. Focus on the main thing–other things will fall into place.

> *One thing I have desired of the Lord,*
> *That will I seek: That I may dwell*
> *in the house of the Lord All the days*
> *of my life, To behold the beauty of the*
> *Lord, And to inquire in His temple.*
>
> Psalm 27:4 (NKJV)

Daily Devotion

Stop trying to please everyone. You can't make everyone like you. You can never do enough to satisfy people. God sent His son, Jesus Christ of Nazareth, who did much for the people by healing their sicknesses and diseases and raising the dead, but they still crucified Him.

Am I now trying to win the approval of human beings, or of God? Or am I trying to please people? If I were still trying to please people, I would not be a servant of Christ.

Galatians 1:10 (NIV)

On the contrary, we speak as those approved by God to be entrusted with the gospel. We are not trying to please people but God, who tests our hearts.

1 Thessalonians 2:4 (NIV)

Work willingly at whatever you do, as though you were working for the Lord rather than for people.

Colossians 3:23 (NLT)

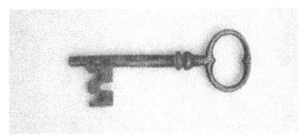

Daily Devotion

Stop dwelling on your past mistakes. You can't change the past, but you can do something about your present, so that you can create a better future. Your past is behind you—your future is ahead of you—and the decisions you make today will influence and impact your future.

> *No, dear brothers and sisters, I have not achieved it, but I focus on this one thing: Forgetting the past and looking forward to what lies ahead,*
>
> Philippians 3:13 (NLT)

> *For if a man belongs to Christ, he is a new person. The old life is gone. New life has begun.*
>
> 2 Corinthians 5:17 (NLV)

73

Daily Devotion

Time is precious; time is essential. If lost, it can never be regained. Time is God's currency on earth given to humanity to do life commerce, so spend your time wisely.

> *How do you know what your life will be like tomorrow? Your life is like the morning fog—it's here a little while, then it's gone.*
>
> James 4:14 (NLT)

> *Walk in wisdom toward those who are outside, redeeming the time.*
>
> Colossians 4:5 (NKJV)

> *Redeeming the time, because the days are evil.*
>
> Ephesians 5:16 (NKJV)

Daily Devotion

Timing is everything. There's a wrong timing and a right timing for everything. Be sensitive and proactive to the circle of time in your life.

There is a time for everything and a season for every activity under the heavens: a time to be born and a time to die, a time to plant and a time to uproot, a time to hill an a time to heal, a time to tear down and a time to build,

Ecclesiastes 3:1-3

Daily Devotion

Sometimes pain comes to remind us of something that is out of order or out of place in our lives—pain is one of our greatest teachers. We learn from our pain: A painful memory helps us to be more cautious and repositions us to create an unforgettable pleasant memory.

*Although the Lord gives you the bread
of adversity and the water of affliction,
your teachers will be hidden no more;
with your own eyes you will see them.*

Isaiah 30:20 (NIV)

*Then I would still have this consolation—
my joy in unrelenting pain—
that I had not denied the
words of the Holy One.*

Job 6:10 (NIV)

76

Daily Devotion

God can get some glory and create a message through your mess. So, get up from your misery and begin to live again. He is the God of another chance.

But this I call to mind, and
therefore I have hope:
The steadfast love of the Lord never ceases;
his mercies never come to an end;
they are new every morning;
great is your faithfulness.

Lamentations 3:21-23 (ESV)

Daily Devotion

If God can get anything to another through you, He will give it to you because He knows he can trust you, that you won't hold back, and that you are determined to be a vessel and a channel of His goodness.

> *Whoever is kind to the poor lends to the Lord,*
> *and he will reward them for*
> *what they have done.*
>
> Proverbs 19:17 (NIV)

Daily Devotion

When you place less value upon yourself, don't expect anyone that comes into your life to raise the price of your true worth.

Look at the birds of the air;
they do not sow or reap or store away in barns,
and yet your heavenly Father feeds them.
Are you not much more valuable than they?

Matthew 6:26 (NIV)

79

Daily Devotion

Always value other people's opinions, even if you don't agree with them, because someday you could benefit from their schools of thought.

> *Elijah went before the people and said,*
> *"How long will you waver*
> *between two opinions?*
> *If the Lord is God, follow him;*
> *but if Baal is God, follow him."*
> *But the people said nothing.*
>
> 1 Kings 18:21 (NIV)

Daily Devotion

Always remember that you are not the only one that's going through tough times. Look around you—there's pain behind every smile and every cute outfit. There were battles fought before every victory, so do not let your pain rob you of your joy.

*Do not grieve,
for the joy of the Lord is your strength.*
Nehemiah 8:10 (NIV)

Daily Devotion

Keep on running, keep on moving, keep on believing. You can't stop now—no one ever stops in the middle of a storm. Live and go through every storm to your breakthrough.

God is our refuge and strength,
an ever-present help in trouble.
Therefore we will not fear,
though the earth give way and
the mountains fall into the heart of the sea,

Psalm 46:1-3 (NIV)

Daily Devotion

Not everyone will be happy for you when they see you succeed. Your victory and blessing sometimes will provoke your enemy to dislike you, so get used to it.

> *But to you who are listening I say:*
> *Love your enemies,*
> *do good to those who hate you.*
> *Bless those who curse you,*
> *pray for those who mistreat you.*
>
> Luke 6:28 (NIV)

Daily Devotion

Always be on the lookout for opportunities. Some opportunities will come once in a lifetime, while others will come in a season. The wisdom and insight to discern a great opportunity is indispensable.

*making the most of every opportunity,
because the days are evil.*

Ephesians 5:16 (NIV)

Daily Devotion

Whenever you find yourself in a season of uncertainty, refrain from making a major decision. Wait for clarity and seek the counsel of the wise before making a move.

*Where no counsel is, the people fall:
but in the multitude of
counsellors there is safety.*

Proverbs 11:14 (KJV)

Daily Devotion

When you experience a financial drought and you desperately desire an unprecedented harvest, get a seed in your hand to activate God's rain of increase from heaven.

> *"As long as the earth endures, seedtime
> and harvest, cold and heat, summer
> and winter, day and night
> will never cease."*
>
> Genesis 8:22 (NIV)

DAILY DEVOTION

There is a future harvest in every seed.

> *Do not be deceived: God cannot be mocked. A man reaps what he sows.*
> Galatians 6:7 (NIV)

Daily Devotion

For every season of supply, always store up enough seed for the next season of famine. You can sow your way out of a season of "just enough" to a season of "more than enough."

> *Then Isaac sowed in that land,*
> *and received in the land in the*
> *same year an hundredfold:*
> *and the Lord blessed him. And*
> *the man waxed great,*
> *and went forward, and grew*
> *until he became very great:*
>
> Gen 26:12-13 (KJV)

Daily Devotion

Seasons of battle always precede seasons of promotion and victory. If there were no battles fought, there would be no victories won. Every battle won takes you to another level of faith to conquer more battles—so keep on fighting.

> *Come to me all you who are*
> *weary and burdened,*
> *and I will give you rest.*
> *Take my yoke upon you and learn from me,*
> *for I am gentle and humble in heart,*
> *and you will find rest for your souls.*
> *For my yoke is easy and my burden is light.*
>
> Matthew 11:28-30 (NIV)

Daily Devotion

Pay attention to every season of struggles and setbacks. There are always lessons to learn from them, and God could also be trying to get your attention to refocus you away from broken focus.

Consider it pure joy, my brothers and sisters, whenever you face trials of many kinds,

James 1:2 (NIV)

Daily Devotion

Sometimes people won't change or get a different perspective in life until the pain of remaining the same supersedes the discomfort of change itself.

> *The way of fools seems right to them,*
> *but the wise listen to advice.*
>
> Proverbs 12:15 (NIV)

> *Only a fool despises his father's advice;*
> *a wise son considers each suggestion.*
>
> Proverbs 15:5 (TLB)

Daily Devotion

Stop focusing and reminiscing on past failures and disappointments. Start celebrating the little victories along the way—it's a new day.

> *Then I saw "a new heaven and a new earth," for the first heaven and the first earth had passed away, and there was no longer any sea. I saw the Holy City, the new Jerusalem, coming down out of heaven from God, prepared as a bride beautifully dressed for her husband. And I heard a loud voice from the throne saying, Look! God's dwelling place is now among the people, and he will dwell with them. They will be his people, and God himself will be with them and be their God.*
>
> Revelation 21:1-3 (NIV)

> *Because of the Lord's great love we are not consumed, for his compassions never fail. They are new every morning; great is your faithfulness.*
>
> Lamentations 3:22-23 (NIV)

But thanks be to God! He gives us the victory through our Lord Jesus Christ.

1 Corinthians 15:57 (NIV)

92

Daily Devotion

Never live your life based on assumptions and lack of understanding. Get the facts and accuracy first. There is always more to how things may appear at first.

Wisdom is the principal thing;
therefore get wisdom:
and with all thy getting get understanding.

Proverbs 4:7 (KJV)

I am sending you out like sheep
with wolves all around you.
Be wise like snakes and gentle like doves.

Matthew 10:16 (NLV)

Daily Devotion

Be patient. Be hopeful. Be prayerful. Be faithful. Be committed. Anyone who has ever achieved anything great has these virtues as their anchor.

> *But as for you, be strong and courageous,*
> *for your work will be rewarded.*
>
> 2 Chronicles 15:7 (NLT)

> *Patient endurance is what you need now,*
> *so that you will continue to do God's will.*
> *Then you will receive all that he has promised.*
>
> Hebrews 10:36 (NLT)

> *I waited patiently for the Lord to help me,*
> *and he turned to me and heard my cry.*
>
> Psalm 40:1 (NLT)

> *Don't worry about anything;*
> *instead, pray about everything.*
> *Tell God what you need,*
> *and thank him for all he has done.*
>
> Philippians 4:6 (NLT)

94

Daily Devotion

When discouragement sets in, faith usually walks out. But knowing your purpose and the reason why you do what you do will give you new energy, new drive, new perspective, and better focus.

> *And it is impossible to please*
> *God without faith.*
> *Anyone who wants to come to*
> *him must believe that*
> *God exists and that he rewards*
> *those who sincerely seek him.*
>
> Hebrews 11:6 (NLT)

> *Have I not commanded you? Be*
> *strong and courageous.*
> *Do not be afraid; do not be discouraged,*
> *for the Lord your God will be*
> *with you wherever you go.*
>
> Joshua 1:9 (NIV)

Daily Devotion

God will not heal anything you conceal. He wants truth revealed so that your total healing and restoration can take place.

*If we confess our sins,
he is faithful and just and
will forgive us our sins
and purify us from all unrighteousness.*

1 John 1:9 (NIV)

*If I regard iniquity in my heart,
the Lord will not hear me:*

Psalm 66:18 (KJV)

96

Daily Devotion

Never despise the days of not enough and the days of trying to get by. Someday the lessons and training learnt in both seasons will be something to treasure.

Do not despise these small beginnings,
for the Lord rejoices to see the work begin,
to see the plumb line in Zerubbabel's hand.

Zechariah 4:10 (NLT)

If you are faithful in little things,
you will be faithful in large ones.
But if you are dishonest in little things,
you won't be honest with
greater responsibilities.

Luke 16:10 (NLT)

97

Daily Devotion

When life gives you sorrow and tears, make the tears your eye lubricant so that you can see clearly to make your next move to your victory and breakthrough.

> *His anger lasts a moment;*
> *his favor lasts for life!*
> *Weeping may go on all night, but*
> *in the morning there is joy.*

Psalm 30:5 (TLB)

Daily Devotion

Never settle for less in life, always strive for more. Strive for the best, aim high enough to shoot for the stars.

*Not that I have already obtained all this,
or have already arrived at my goal,
but I press on to take hold of that for
which Christ Jesus took hold of me.*
Philippians 3:12 (NIV)

Daily Devotion

Winners don't quit and failures do not stick around. Be determined to be a winner. You will never win until you can conceive the idea of winning in your mind.

*No, in all these things we are more
than conquerors through him who loved us.*

Romans 8:37 (NIV)

*But thanks be to God! He gives us the
victory through our Lord Jesus Christ.*

1 Corinthians 15:57 (NIV)

Daily Devotion

Decide to be on the giving side in any relationship. Give more than you receive without keeping any record of your giving. This practice will eliminate your self-centeredness and selfishness. It will also keep you from being emotionally hurt over unrealistic expectation from the other party.

*And I was a constant example
to you in helping the poor;
for I remembered the words of the Lord Jesus,
'It is more blessed to give than to receive.*

Acts 20:35 (TLB)

*And here is how to measure
it—the greatest love is
shown when a person lays down
his life for his friends;*

John 15:13 (TLB)

Daily Devotion

Never underestimate the gifts and potentials that God has deposited in you. You might not be called to everyone, but there's definitely someone out there to whom your message is tailored to.

*Do not neglect your gift,
which was given you through prophecy
when the body of elders laid their hands on you.*

1 Timothy 4:14 (NIV)

*But we have this treasure in jars of clay
to show that this all-surpassing power
is from God and not from us.*

2 Corinthians 4:7 (NIV)

102

Daily Devotion

Your memory will always remind you of the past, but your imagination will create and design a future for you to gravitate towards. So, use your imagination more; it is a powerful tool.

David did, and defeated Goliath by using his memory from slaying the bear and the lion, and his imagination of his victory ahead over Goliath.

*But David said to Saul,
Your servant has been keeping
his father's sheep.
When a lion or a bear came and
carried off a sheep from the flock,
I went after it, struck it and rescued
the sheep from its mouth.
When it turned on me, I seized it by its hair,
struck it and killed it.
Your servant has killed both
the lion and the bear;
this uncircumcised Philistine
will be like one of them,
because he has defied the armies
of the living God.*

1 Samuel 17:34-36 (NIV)

103

DAILY DEVOTION

You are the sum total of your imagination. We eventually become what we imagine the most, good or bad, so think big and imagine good thoughts.

For as he thinks in his heart so is he.
Proverbs 23:7 (NKJV)

Daily Devotion

Always have a reason to trust and believe in people until they prove otherwise. Stop penalizing Jack for Bobby's actions and wrongdoings in your relationships. Learn to give people the space and room to grow.

> *it does not rejoice at wrongdoing, but rejoices with the truth. Love bears all things, believes all things, hopes all things, endures all things.*
>
> 1 Corinthians 13:6-7 (ESV)

Daily Devotion

Refrain from being selfish with your love. Never hold back from showing affection to the people that are dear to you because of past hurt or grudges. Life is too short—they could be gone tomorrow and then it will be too late to express your love to them.

*Love is patient, love is kind. It does not envy,
it does not boast, it is not proud. It does not
dishonor others, it is not self-seeking, it is not
easily angered, it keeps no record of wrongs.
Love does not delight in evil but rejoices
with the truth. It always protects, always
trusts, always hopes, always perseveres.*

1 Corinthians 13:4-7 (NIV)

Daily Devotion

Sometimes God will use delays, detours, and exits to redefine motives, purpose, and agenda on your road to destiny.

*And we know that in all things God works
for the good of those who love him, who have
been called according to his purpose.*

Romans 8:28 (NIV)

*For I know the plans I have for
you, declares the Lord,
plans to prosper you and not to harm you,
plans to give you hope and a future.*

Jeremiah 29:11 (NIV)

*For my thoughts are not your thoughts,
neither are your ways my ways, declares the Lord.
As the heavens are higher than the earth,
so are my ways higher than your ways
and my thoughts than your thoughts.*

Isaiah 55:8-9 (NIV)

Daily Devotion

Keep your expectations of people realistic. If you set them too high, you will be disappointed and feel let down.

*Even my close friend, someone I trusted,
one who shared my bread, has
turned against me.*

Psalm 41:9 (NIV)

*Some trust in chariots and some in horses,
but we trust in the name of the Lord our God.*

Psalm 20:7 (NIV)

*All my intimate friends detest me;
those I love have turned against me.*

Job 19:19 (NIV)

Daily Devotion

Sometimes God will let you exhaust all human options before He'll reveal heaven's best to you because He longs for your total dependency upon Him.

> *I lift up my eyes to the mountains—*
> *where does my help come from?*
> *My help comes from the Lord,*
> *the Maker of heaven and earth.*

Psalm 121:1-2 (NIV)

> *My flesh and my heart may fail,*
> *but God is the strength of my heart*
> *and my portion forever.*

Psalm 73:26 (NIV)

> *For I am the Lord your God*
> *who takes hold of your right hand and says to you,*
> *Do not fear; I will help you.*

Isaiah 41:13 (NIV)

109

Daily Devotion

Never put off today's assignment for tomorrow's daydreaming and fantasy—"should have, could have, would have" is your vision's greatest enemy—so stop procrastinating and do it now.

> *Whoever watches the wind will not plant;*
> *whoever looks at the clouds will not reap.*
>
> Ecclesiastes 11:4 (NIV)

> *Lazy hands make for poverty,*
> *but diligent hands bring wealth.*
>
> Proverbs 10:4 (NIV)

> *Diligent hands will rule,*
> *but laziness ends in forced labor.*
>
> Proverbs 12:24 (NIV)

Daily Devotion

Your situation is not that bad, so cheer up. Stop complaining because you cannot afford another pair of Jordan shoes. Remember that someone else has a worse situation—maybe they just had their leg amputated due to an illness. Always give thanks with a grateful heart.

> *Let them give thanks to the Lord for his unfailing love and his wonderful deeds for mankind, for he satisfies the thirsty and fills the hungry with good things.*
>
> Psalm 107:8-9 (NIV)

> *I will give thanks to you, Lord, with all my heart; I will tell of all your wonderful deeds.*
>
> Psalm 9:1 (NIV)

Daily Devotion

Always give yourself enough time to plan and schedule events in your life ahead of time. Last minute improvisation always creates some level of chaos, uncertainty, and flawed results.

*A wise man thinks ahead;
a fool doesn't and even brags about it!*

Proverbs 13:16 (TLB)

*Prepare your work outside;
get everything ready for yourself in the field,
and after that build your house.*

Proverbs 24:27 (ESV)

Daily Devotion

Never accept praise from an enemy—it is a trap and a set up to draw you close and scrutinize your life for greater attacks. Remember those that say "Hosanna!" today have the tendency to say "Crucify him" tomorrow.

> *Be careful—watch out for attacks from Satan,*
> *your great enemy. He prowls*
> *around like a hungry,*
> *roaring lion, looking for some*
> *victim to tear apart.*
>
> 1 Peter 5:8 (TLB)

Daily Devotion

Whenever you open up your hand to give and not withhold, God opens up the windows of heaven to pour out and release blessings upon you.

> *Give, and it will be given to you.*
> *Good measure, pressed down,*
> *shaken together, running over,*
> *will be put into your lap.*
> *For with the measure you use*
> *it will be measured back to you.*

Luke 6:38 (ESV)

Daily Devotion

You will never find time for anything until you create time for something. The proof of your desire is found in what you give your time to.

*making the best use of the time,
because the days are evil*

Ephesians 5:16 (ESV)

*yet you do not know what tomorrow will bring.
What is your life? For you are a mist
that appears for a little time and then vanishes.*

James 4:14 (ESV)

Daily Devotion

Do not fall for the pressure of living up to people's expectations. Instead, stay committed to building godly character. A godly character will always stand the test of time and will not disappoint you.

> *Have nothing to do with godless*
> *myths and old wives' tales;*
> *rather, train yourself to be godly.*
> *For physical training is of some value,*
> *but godliness has value for all things,*
> *holding promise for both the present life*
> *and the life to come.*
>
> 1 Timothy 4:7-8 (NIV)

116

Daily Devotion

Whenever you think of giving up or throwing in the towel, first think of those that will be disappointed by your action. Also think of those who could stop believing because they believed in you—those that could stop reaching for their destinies because you gave up on yours. You were born to impact your world.

> *Therefore, since we are surrounded*
> *by such a great cloud of witnesses,*
> *let us throw off everything that hinders*
> *and the sin that so easily entangles.*
> *And let us run with perseverance*
> *the race marked out for us,*
>
> Hebrews 12:1 (NIV)

> *But as for you, be strong and do not give up,*
> *for your work will be rewarded.*
>
> 2 Chronicles 15:7 (NIV)

Daily Devotion

Your greatest pain will inevitably produce your greatest miracle. No pain–no gain. There's always a miracle on the other side of every pain and struggle.

*Therefore we do not lose heart.
Though outwardly we are wasting away,
yet inwardly we are being renewed day by day.
For our light and momentary
troubles are achieving for us
an eternal glory that far outweighs them all.
So we fix our eyes not on what is seen,
but on what is unseen,
since what is seen is temporary,
but what is unseen is eternal.*

2 Corinthians 4:16-18 (NIV)

*weeping may stay for the night,
but rejoicing comes in the morning.*

Psalm 30:5 (NIV)

Daily Devotion

If you begin to consider your resources at hand before launching out, your faith may never have the opportunity to be activated. Stepping out of the boat with nothing is a proof of your faith.

Faith without works is dead.
James 2:14 (KJV)

Daily Devotion

Always do what you can, while you can, when you can, with whatever you have at any given moment. Don't let the moment pass you by but seize every opportunity—maximize every moment. You may not get the chance again.

*making the most of every opportunity,
because the days are evil.*

Ephesians 5:16 (NIV)

*As long as it is day, we must
do the works of him
who sent me. Night is coming,
when no one can work.*

John 9:4 (NIV)

120

Daily Devotion

Dare to cultivate the spirit of a finisher. Stopping halfway and procrastinating on your vision or any project will only lead you to an endless parade of failure and unaccomplished goals and dreams.

*And Jesus said unto him,
No man, having put his hand to the plough,
and looking back, is fit for the kingdom of God.*

Luke 9:62 (KJV)

*Now finish the work, so that
your eager willingness
to do it may be matched by
your completion of it,
according to your means.*

Corinthians 8:11 (NIV)

*I have fought the good fight,
I have finished the race,
I have kept the faith.*

2 Timothy 4:7 (NIV)

Daily Devotion

Sometimes a new season in your life will require you to welcome new relationships. Those that embraced and celebrated you in the past might not necessarily embrace your new season. People come and go when their season is over in the relationship. Freely let go and be at peace in your heart.

The Lord's loving kindness indeed never cease,
For His compassion never fails.
They are new every morning;
Great is Your faithfulness.

Lamentations 3:22-23 (NASB)

To everything there is a season,
and a time to every purpose under the heaven:

Ecclesiastes 3:1 (KJV)

And we know that all things work together
for good to them that love God,
to them who are the called
according to his purpose.

Romans 8:28 (KJV)

Daily Devotion

Ideas are like people—they come and go. An idea that you were passionate about in one season could change in another season. So, stay in touch with your intuition and instinct.

> *I now do according to your word.*
> *Indeed I give you a wise and discerning mind;*
> *no one like you has been before you*
> *and no one like you shall arise after you.*
>
> 1 Kings 3:12 (NRSV)

Daily Devotion

Train your mind to think something new each day. It will give you new energy and open your mind to creativity. Remember you have the creative nature of God in you because you were created in His own image and likeness.

*For we are God's handiwork,
created in Christ Jesus to do good works,
which God prepared in advance for us to do.*

Ephesians 2:10 (NIV)

*Whatever you do,
work at it with all your heart,
as working for the Lord,
not for human masters,*

Colossians 3:23 (NIV)

Daily Devotion

Do not let your dreams and ideas stay too long in your thought realm before launching them—otherwise they will evaporate like vapor. Do something about them today.

Whatever your hand finds to do,
do it with all your might,
for in the realm of the dead,
where you are going,
there is neither working nor planning
nor knowledge nor wisdom.

Ecclesiastes 9:10 (NIV)

125

Daily Devotion

Always relentlessly pursue whatever vision or passion that you are passionate about at every season of your life. You'll never accomplish anything that you are not passionate about.

Passion is what separates winners from losers.

> *Never be lacking in zeal,*
> *but keep your spiritual fervor,*
> *serving the Lord.*
>
> Romans 12:11 (NIV)

> *Not slothful in business;*
> *fervent in spirit;*
> *serving the Lord;*
>
> Romans 12:11 (KJV)

Daily Devotion

No one could ever understand the load you carry nor the burdens you bear because they are not in your shoes. So, stop expecting their sympathy; be at peace with their apathy. Lay your burdens upon the Lord.

*Cast all your anxiety on him
because he cares for you.*

1 Peter 5:7 (NIV)

127

Daily Devotion

Taking too long to decide on something, sitting on the fence, and being indecisive could rob you of your potential and your ability to go to the next level.

But let him ask in faith, nothing wavering.
For he that wavereth is like a wave of the sea
driven with the wind and tossed.
For let not that man think that he shall
receive any thing of the Lord.
A double minded man is
unstable in all his ways.

James 1:6-8 (KJV)

128

Daily Devotion

The strength of an army general is proven in the battlefield. Your battles and tribulation only reveal your true strength.

If you faint in the day of adversity,
thy strength is small.

Proverbs 24:10 (ASV)

Daily Devotion

Your moral weaknesses and flaws are like another individual living on the inside of you. If you don't destroy them, they will destroy you.

> *Do not conform to the pattern of this world,*
> *but be transformed by the*
> *renewing of your mind.*
> *Then you will be able to test and*
> *approve what God's will is—*
> *his good, and pleasing and perfect will.*
>
> Romans 12:2 (NIV)

Daily Devotion

You will never conquer the enemy you refuse to confront. Anything you consistently allow in your life will eventually dominate you and permanently find a place in your heart.

*Whoever conceals their sins does not prosper,
but the one who confesses and
renounces them finds mercy.*

Proverbs 28:13 (NIV)

*If we confess our sins,
he is faithful and just and
will forgive us our sins
and purify us from all unrighteousness.*

1 John 1:9 (NIV)

Daily Devotion

Refuse to go through this life unfulfilled. Discover your eternal purpose and assignment, and you will find fulfillment. You can choose to learn from someone, but you cannot live their life—you must live your life. Let God lead you to find your path.

*And we know that in all things God works
for the good of those who love him,
who have been called according to his purpose.*

Romans 8:28 (NIV)

Daily Devotion

You will never discover the greatness in you and your own potential if you keep wishing you were someone else. You are unique, so embrace you and God in you.

*We do not dare to classify or compare ourselves
with some who commend themselves.
When they measure themselves by themselves
and compare themselves with themselves,
they are not wise.*

2 Corinthians 10:12 (NIV)

*For you created my inmost being;
you knit me together in my mother's womb.*

Psalm 139:13 (NIV)

Daily Devotion

Stop looking at where you've been [your past], stop considering staying where you are [your present], and start envisioning where you would rather be [a better future].

*There is surely a future hope for you,
and your hope will not be cut off.*

Proverbs 23:18 (NIV)

Daily Devotion

Never be content with being "just okay" in life. Always demand excellence and the very best out of yourself. Always push yourself beyond your limitation—become your own strongest competitor.

*Therefore I do not run like
someone running aimlessly;
I do not fight like a boxer beating the air.
No, I strike a blow to my body
and make it my slave
so that after I have preached to others,
I myself will not be disqualified for the prize.*

1 Corinthians 9:26-27 (NIV)

Daily Devotion

Never underestimate the power of little details. Pay attention to them because little acorns can become mighty oak trees.

> *He replied, Because you have so little faith.*
> *Truly I tell you,*
> *if you have faith as small as a mustard seed,*
> *you can say to this mountain,*
> *'Move from here to there,'*
> *and it will move.*
> *Nothing will be impossible for you.*

Matthew 17:20 (NIV)

Daily Devotion

One of the greatest battles in life is the battle in your mind—so renew your mind daily with the Word of God.

*Do not conform to the pattern of this world,
but be transformed by the
renewing of your mind.
Then you will be able to test and
approve what God's will is—
his good, and pleasing and perfect will.*

Romans 12:2 (NIV)

Daily Devotion

When what used to work for you stops working for you, let go and let God give you new direction. Do not get hung up on what used to be. Our God is a God of new creativity; He is always doing something new.

See I am doing a new thing!
Now it springs up; do you not perceive it?
I am making a way in the wilderness
and streams in the wasteland.

Isaiah 43:19 (NIV)

Daily Devotion

Pleasant and unpleasant situations will always come and go in your life. Don't allow them to be the determining factors for your emotional stability.

> *Set your minds on things above,*
> *not on earthly things.*
>
> Colossians 3:2 (NIV)

139

Daily Devotion

Never give anyone the key to your emotional stability—otherwise they'll lock you down and put a lid of limitation over you.

*I pray that out of his glorious riches
he may strengthen you with power
through his Spirit in your inner being,*

Ephesians 3:16 (NIV)

*Now I take limitations in stride,
and with good cheer,
these limitations that cut me down to size—
abuse, accidents, opposition, bad breaks.
I just let Christ take over!
And so the weaker I get, the stronger I become.*

2 Corinthians 12:10 (MSG)

Daily Devotion

Manipulation is always driven by greed, self-centeredness, and lack of self-fulfillment deep down on the inside. Always strive to put others before you and it will create a sense of worthiness on the inside of you.

> *then make my joy complete*
> *by being like-minded,*
> *having the same love, being one*
> *in spirit and of one mind.*
> *Do nothing out of selfish*
> *ambition or vain conceit.*
> *Rather, in humility value*
> *others above yourselves,*
> *not looking to your own interests*
> *but each of you to the interests of the others.*
> *In your relationships with one another,*
> *have the same mindset as Christ Jesus:*

Philippians 2:2-5 (NIV)

Daily Devotion

You will never find inner peace and self-fulfillment if you constantly harbor resentment and bitterness in your heart. Be quick to forgive. You cannot spend the rest of your life in bitterness and unforgiveness. It will hold you bound and eat you up like cancer. Release those you need to release and let them go, so that you can move on with your life.

> *And whenever you stand praying, forgive,*
> *if you have anything against anyone,*
> *so that your Father also who is in heaven*
> *may forgive you of your trespasses.*
>
> Mark 11:25 (ESV)

Daily Devotion

Do not let a temporary emotional feeling disrupt your pursuit of your life's goal and visions. Keep your head up high. Feelings are temporary. Do not let your feelings dictate your focus.

> *Why, my soul, are you downcast?*
> *Why so disturbed within me?*
> *Put your hope in God,*
> *for I will yet praise him,*
> *my Savior and my God.*
>
> Psalm 42:5 (NIV)

143

Daily Devotion

Be patient and hopeful even when the road to your destiny becomes cloudy and rocky. Do not become discouraged. Stay positive and optimistic. Avoid speaking negativity into your situation. Speak life and not death.

> *Then he said to me, "Prophesy to*
> *these bones and say to them,*
> *'Dry bones, hear the word of the Lord!*
> *This is what the Sovereign*
> *Lord says to these bones:*
> *I will make breath enter you,*
> *and you will come to life.*
> *I will attach tendons to you and*
> *make flesh come upon you*
> *and cover you with skin; I*
> *will put breath in you,*
> *and you will come to life.*
> *Then you will know that I am the Lord.'"*

Ezekiel 37:4-6 (NIV)

Daily Devotion

The reason a vision is called a vision is because of your ability to see it happen in your mind and in your spirit before it becomes a reality.

> *He brought him outside and said,*
> *Look up toward heaven and count the stars,*
> *if you are able to count them.*
> *And He said to him,*
> *So will your descendants be.*
>
> Genesis 15:5 (MEV)

Daily Devotion

The reason why sometimes people can't identify with your passion is because they haven't perceived what you have perceived, or conceived what you have conceived. They also might not have your rhythm or instinct, so be at peace with it.

> *Can two walk together,*
> *except they be agreed?*
> Amos 3:3 (KJV)

Daily Devotion

Life is too short, so be determined to live it to its fullest with all that lies within you. Pursue peace, joy, fun, and good times instead of chaos and complication.

> *A cheerful heart is good medicine,*
> *but a crushed spirit dries up the bones.*
> Proverbs 17:22 (NIV)

147

Daily Devotion

Never live your life in uncertainty. Plan and design every road map that will lead you from here to there. Never let your "there" take you unaware. Cherish every moment of your journey. Moments becomes seasons! Seasons becomes years! Years becomes decades! Decades becomes eternity!

*The plans of the diligent lead to profit
as surely as haste leads to poverty.*

Proverbs 21:5 (NIV)

*Go to the ant, you sluggard;
consider its ways and be wise!
It has no commander, no overseer or ruler,
yet it stores its provisions in summer
and gathers its food at harvest.*

Proverbs 6:6-8 (NIV)

*Put your outdoor work in order
and get your fields ready;
after that, build your house.*

Proverbs 24:27 (NIV)

148

Daily Devotion

Discover the environment in which you thrive while you are in it. Always strive to create the right environment because it could be the bedrock of the emergence of your inspiration and creativity. If waterfalls and peaceful tranquility songs set you in the mood of relaxation, or if listening to instrumental jazz music tends to soothe your soul, then go for it.

I have told you these things,
so that in me you may have peace.
In this world you will have trouble.
But take heart! I have overcome the world.

John 16:33 (NIV)

Return to your rest, my soul,
for the Lord has been good to you.

Psalm 116:7 (NIV)

149

Daily Devotion

Do not let someone else's opinion, nonchalant attitude, or pessimism influence you negatively or keep you from pursuing your life's goal and vision.

*Commit to the Lord whatever you do,
and he will establish your plans.*

Proverbs 16:3 (NIV)

*And the Lord answered me:
Write the vision; make it plain upon tablets,
so he may run who reads it.*

Habakkuk 2:2 (RSV)

150

Daily Devotion

You were supposed to learn a valuable lesson from your past mistakes. It wasn't meant to take you through a lifetime of torture and endless parade of regrets.

As a dog returns to its vomit,
so a fool returns to his folly.
Do you see a man wise in his own conceit?
There is more hope for a fool than for him.

Proverbs 26:11-12 (MEV)

Do not remember the former things
nor consider the things of old.

Isaiah 43:18 (MEV)

Daily Devotion

Life without balance always leaves an area of your life to suffer, which then leads to a lack of wholeness, a life of pressure, and feelings of unfulfillment and emptiness. So, work hard, but also find some time to unwind and rejuvenate.

> *Come to Me, all you who*
> *labor and are heavily burdened,*
> *and I will give you rest.*
> *Take My yoke upon you, and learn from Me.*
> *For I am meek and lowly in heart,*
> *and you will find rest for your souls.*
> *For My yoke is easy, and My burden is light.*
>
> Matthew 11:28-30 (MEV)

> *It is in vain for you to rise up early,*
> *to stay up late,*
> *and to eat the bread of hard toil,*
> *for He gives sleep to His beloved.*
>
> Psalm 127:2 (MEV)

*Then He said to them,
Come away by yourselves to a remote place
and rest a while,
for many were coming and going,
and they had no leisure even to eat.*

Mark 6:31 (MEV)

152

Daily Devotion

Never wish you had someone else's kind of lifestyle. You don't know what it cost them to be them. There may also be things in their success package that you do not want.

Rest in the Lord, and wait patiently for Him;
do not fret because of those who
prosper in their way,
because of those who make wicked schemes.

Psalm 37:7 (MEV)

Daily Devotion

Every new challenge in life always opens a door for you to learn something new. Some challenges are walls you must conquer and break down through endurance and faithfulness, while other challenges could simply be doors you must humbly walk through to get to the next level.

*But after you have suffered a little while,
the God of all grace,
who has called us to His eternal
glory through Christ Jesus,
will restore, support, strengthen,
and establish you.*

1 Peter 5:10 (MEV)

*We are troubled on every
side, yet not distressed;
we are perplexed, but not in despair;
persecuted, but not forsaken;
cast down, but not destroyed;*

2 Corinthians 4:8-9 (MEV)

Daily Devotion

Success will only come to those who are relentless and willing to pay the ultimate price and sacrifice to distinguish themselves from others.

*Therefore, my dear brothers
and sisters, stand firm.
Let nothing move you.
Always give yourselves fully to
the work of the Lord,
because you know that your labor
in the Lord is not in vain.*

1 Corinthians 15:58 (NIV)

*But we do not belong to those
who shrink back and
are destroyed, but to those who
have faith and are saved.*

Hebrews 10:39 (NIV)

Daily Devotion

Become your own number one cheerleader. Always believe in yourself, even if others don't believe in you.

> *And David's two wives were taken captives,*
> *Ahinoam the Jezreelitess, and*
> *Abigail the wife of Nabal the Carmelite.*
> *And David was greatly distressed;*
> *for the people spake of stoning him,*
> *because the soul of all the people was grieved,*
> *every man for his sons and for his daughters:*
> *but David encouraged himself*
> *in the Lord his God.*
>
> 1 Samuel 30:5-6 (KJV)

156

Daily Devotion

Always strive to be your own strongest competitor. Always push yourself beyond every limitation. Make it a habit to always demand excellence out of yourself all the time.

*Have I not commanded you? Be
strong and courageous.
Do not be afraid; do not be discouraged,
for the Lord your God will be
with you wherever you go.*

Joshua 1:9 (NIV)

*Not that I have already obtained all this,
or have already arrived at my goal,
but I press on to take hold of that
for which Christ Jesus took hold of me.*

Philippians 3:12 (NIV)

Daily Devotion

Avoid shortcuts to your destiny. Shortcuts always end up robbing you of process and creativity along the way. There's no easy way to greatness; take the steps and stop looking for elevators to greatness. Steps will give you a solid foundation.

Commit to the Lord whatever you do,
and he will establish your plans.

Proverbs 16:3 (NIV)

The plans of the diligent lead to profit
as surely as haste leads to poverty.

Proverbs 21:5 (NIV)

Daily Devotion

Do not let the success of another man's assignment and vision intimidate or stop you from pursuing yours. Our giftings are different in many ways.

> *Each of you should use whatever gift you have received to serve others, as faithful stewards of God's grace in its various forms.*
>
> 1 Peter 4:10 (NIV)

> *We have different gifts,*
> *according to the grace given to each of us.*
> *If your gift is prophesying,*
> *then prophesy in accordance with your faith;*
> *if it is serving, then serve;*
> *if it is teaching, then teach;*
> *if it is to encourage, then give encouragement;*
> *if it is giving, then give generously;*
> *if it is to lead, do it diligently;*
> *if it is to show mercy, do it cheerfully.*
>
> Romans 12:6-8 (NIV)

*To one he gave five bags of gold,
to another two bags,
and to another one bag,
each according to his ability.
Then he went on his journey.*

Matthew 25:15 (NIV)

Daily Devotion

In order to know someone better, always ask them questions, even if you think you may already know the answers to the questions you are asking. It will help reveal who they truly are and any ulterior motives.

Therefore judge nothing before the appointed time;
wait until the Lord comes.
He will bring to light what is hidden in darkness
and will expose the motives of the heart.
At that time each will receive
their praise from God.

1 Corinthians 4:5 (NIV)

But the Lord said to Samuel,
Do not consider his appearance or his height,
for I have rejected him.
The Lord does not look at the things people look at.
People look at the outward appearance,
but the Lord looks at the heart.

1 Samuel 16:7 (NIV)

160

DAILY DEVOTION

Always find a way to make up for a promise that you failed to keep. Be credible and always value the integrity of your words.

*A person who promises a gift but doesn't give it
is like clouds and wind that bring no rain.*

Proverbs 25:14 (NLT)

*Don't make rash promises,
and don't be hasty in bringing
matters before God.
After all, God is in heaven,
and you are here on earth.
So let your words be few.*

Ecclesiastes 5:2 (NLT)

161

Daily Devotion

Those who quit have a 0% chance of succeeding, but those who keep working out their visions and dreams have a 99.9% chance of succeeding.

*Do you not know that in a
race all the runners run,
but only one receives the prize?
So run that you may obtain it.*

1 Corinthians 9:24 (ESV)

Daily Devotion

A man without a plan is like a sailor without a sea to sail, like a traveler without a road map or destination, like a leader without a vision. You will live well if you plan well.

> *The plans of the diligent lead*
> *surely to abundance,*
> *but everyone who is hasty*
> *comes only to poverty.*
>
> Proverbs 21:5 (ESV)

> *The heart of man plans his way,*
> *but the Lord establishes his steps.*
>
> Proverbs 16:9 (ESV)

> *Go to the ant, O lazy person.*
> *Watch and think about her ways, and be wise.*
> *She has no leader, head or ruler,*
> *but she gets her food ready in the summer,*
> *and gathers her food at the right time.*
> *How long will you lie down, O lazy person?*
> *When will you rise up from your sleep?*

*A little sleep, a little rest,
a little folding of the hands to rest,
and being poor will come
upon you like a robber,
and your need like a man ready to fight.*

Proverbs 6:6-11 (NLV)

ABOUT THE AUTHOR

Pastor Keith Banks-Obanor [AKA, PK] is the Lead Pastor of Victory World Church Int'l in Canton, Massachusetts and the founder of Victory World Outreach Ministries, which is an outreach organization—reaching and touching lives—extending its impact to nations like Uganda, Kenya & Nigeria. He is also the host of 'VICTORY TODAY'.

Pastor Banks obtained his ministerial education from LoveWorld Ministerial College under Pastor Chris Oyakhilome, Lagos, Nigeria, and also from Gordon-Conwell Theological Seminary, Boston, Massachusetts. His messages and writings are full of faith, hope, and the anointing that transcends boundaries and limitations—to recreate and change your world. Pastor Keith is a prolific author and teacher of the Word who operates dynamically in the prophetic and healing anointing. He is CEO of Aspire Holdings and Acquisitions. His authority in the Word of God always creates a momentum for breakthrough. He is a member in good standing of the City Harvest Network under the pastoral covering and leadership of Dr. Rod Parsley, World Harvest Church in Columbus Ohio. He is also a member of 'A Church Without Walls', Boston, Massachusetts, under the spiritual covering and presbytery of Bishop G.A Thompson. He is married to his choir sweetheart, Senior Pastor, and 1st Lady Sogie Cynthia Banks-Obanor. They are blessed with three lovely children—Charisma, Sharon, and Joey.

CONTACT INFORMATION FOR BOOKING

Email all request to EstherPRO.vwc@gmail.com or Pk.victoryworld@gmail.com

@pkvictoryworld

www.ingramcontent.com/pod-product-compliance
Lightning Source LLC
Chambersburg PA
CBHW070059080526
44586CB00013B/1121